MINDFULNESS FOR BEGINNERS

How to Live in the Moment, Stress and Worry Free, in a Constant State of Peace and Happiness

Yesenia Chavan

D0283319

Evita Publishing, PO Box 306, Station A, Vancouver Island, BC V9W 5B1 Canada

Table of Contents

Chapter 9

Introduction

Thank you for purchasing my book *Mindfulness for Beginners: How to Live in the Moment, Stress and Worry Free, in a Constant State of Peace and Happiness.* Also, congratulations for being willing to learn more about mindfulness in order to make it a part of your daily life.

With *Mindfulness for Beginners* you're going to learn exactly how to be mindful, how to use mindfulness techniques to quiet your mind, and how to practice mindfulness every day in order to gain control of your life.

Learning how to be mindful and developing a regular mindfulness practice can be a challenge at first because our "monkey minds," as Buddhists call them, jump from thought to thought like monkeys swinging from tree to tree. If our minds aren't tossing around regrets of the past, they're busy fearing the future.

Practicing mindfulness, however, can make you happier, healthier, and more productive than ever. This book will show you how to tame your monkey mind, stop worrying, relieve stress, and embrace a more peaceful way of living.

If you want to change your life you can only do that in the present moment with the thoughts you choose to think. If you can develop the habit of practicing mindfulness, even just for a few minutes each day, you can achieve amazing results in your life. *Mindfulness for Beginners* will walk you through exactly how to use mindfulness to achieve personal success.

Mindfulness will improve your physical and mental health, reduce stress, improve your clarity and focus, and give you a deep sense of peace. When you're run down, stressed out, and anxious, your ability to enjoy life gets depleted.

Mindfulness is an elevated state of being that enables you to rise above your circumstances and experience a sense of joy. As you experience joy, you attract health, finances, abundance, and a slew of other wonderful things into your life.

You were never meant to feel stuck, burnt out, and unhappy. Thank you for allowing me to help you free yourself with mindfulness today!

Chapter 1

What is Mindfulness?

"Mindfulness means paying attention in a particular way: on purpose, in the present moment, and non-judgmentally. This kind of attention nurtures greater awareness, clarity and acceptance of present-moment reality."
Dr. Jon Kabat-Zinn

The History and Definition of Mindfulness

Buddhism referenced the concept of mindfulness over 2500 years ago. The word "mindfulness" comes from the Pali language which was indigenous to the Indian subcontinent.

The word "mindfulness" is a combination of the Pali words "Sati" and "Sampajana." These two words when put together translate to mean awareness, discernment, circumspection, and retention.

Linguistic scholars that studied these terms defined mindfulness as *remembering to have a caring and discerning moment-to-moment awareness of what is happening in ones immediate reality.*

When the concept of mindfulness was first introduced to Western science it was thought that mindfulness, along with the meditation practices it encourages was connected to religious beliefs and therefore only attainable by a select group of people.

Several decades later these myths were dispelled and Western science came to understand mindfulness as an inbred aspect of human consciousness. That is, an inherent ability to be aware of the present moment.

The most common Western definition of mindfulness is by Dr. Jon Kabat-Zinn, one of the main founders of the field of mindfulness. His definition of mindfulness is "paying attention in a particular way: on purpose, in the present moment, and non-judgmentally."

Mindfulness can also be understood by contrasting the word with its opposite, *mindlessness*. Mindlessness is when awareness and attention is scattered and unfocused due to a preoccupation with worry, the past, or the future. Mindlessness causes limited attention and awareness to what's going on in the present moment thus depleting ones power to live the present day to the fullest.

Understanding Mindfulness

We live in a busy world. Men and women everywhere are up at the crack of dawn rushing through breakfast, chatting on the phone and answering emails .Families are stuck on a 24/7 merry-go-round of work, school, after school activities, appointments etc.

When the day finally winds down, most people zone out in front of the television for some much needed down time.

Yet days come and go and the rush of accomplishing an endless list of "to-do's" often leaves people lacking a connection with the present moment – missing out on the special moments that lie within what they are doing.

Living on "automatic pilot" becomes the norm for most people. Sure they're alive but they're not really living each moment. It's kind of like sleepwalking. They go through the motions but somehow seem absent from their own life.

On automatic pilot the brain becomes a plethora of thoughts that skip from one unfinished idea to another. Each thought

10

rudely and obnoxiously interrupts another with a jumble of questions, answers, pondering and arguing all of which are overlapped with endless pictures, ideas, desires and memories.

Mindfulness is a way of reconnecting with life itself. It is a form of self-awareness that allows one to take a step back from the noise of the mind and observe the mental activity and the feelings it generates. By doing this it is possible to separate oneself from the influence of an overactive, 'on automatic pilot' mind.

The Key Ingredients of Mindfulness

Freedom from the chaos of mental activity

Freedom to live in the present moment

Freedom from judgment

Freedom from attachment

Freedom from the chaos of mental activity

Mindfulness enables you to be an "observer" of your thoughts and feelings rather than a victim of them. The chaos of mental activity has no purpose other than to make you a prisoner of its perpetual circle of craziness.

When you learn to be mindful, you learn how to relax and act as a witness of your inner life. You become free from the negative effects of mental chaos and free from judging yourself, others and the world at large.

As you begin to master "observation," you begin to live in the moment and not on autopilot. The more you do this, the more you come to experience relaxation, stillness and a sense of freedom.

Freedom to live in the present moment

Freedom to live in the present moment simply means that you apply the fullness of your conscious awareness to each moment. Freely experiencing each moment stops you from dividing your conscious awareness between today and yesterday as well as today and tomorrow.

Buddha himself said "The secret of health for both mind and body is not to mourn for the past, worry about the future, or anticipate troubles, but to live in the present moment wisely and earnestly."

Freedom from judgment

Being free from judgment simply means that you do not attach your opinions to the happenings of the present moment but rather act as an independent observer without disturbing them by your preferences and prejudices.

Opinions, preferences and prejudices are based on judgments using criteria from past experiences. They are thus stale and therefore cannot be applied to the freshness of the present moment.

When you are mindful, you consciously stay alert and attentive to each moment. Instead of judging things as "good" or "bad" you simply acknowledge and accept them without judgment. This enables you to be freed from reacting to the events and circumstances around you that are often beyond your control.

When you live on autopilot, your reactions, thoughts and feelings just happen to you without you having any say in the matter. When you are attentive and mindful of the present moment, you respond to things with acceptance and openness.

Mindfulness allows you to choose how you will react to events and experiences in your life. If you choose to judge an event, even though mindfulness teaches you not to judge, then your judgment of the event will only be useless and harmful to you.

For example, if your judgment of an event causes you to boil over with anger, then all you have done is boil over with anger. The fact that you're angry is useless. It doesn't change the situation and neither does it benefit the situation. All it does is cause you bodily harm because it creates stress.

Buddha said "You will not be punished for your anger; you will be punished *by* your anger."

When you choose to remain free from judgment, you accept things as they are. You look at "what is" and accept it as such.

Living life free from judgment allows you to control your state of mind in every moment and in every situation.

Freedom from attachment

It is easy to remain attached to old views and wrong perceptions that you've had for a long time. This type of narrow-mindedness forces negative, useless perceptions and opinions onto the events of the present moment.

Attachment is closely related to judgment because it is a personal opinion that you use to assess the happenings of the moment. In order to live in a state of mindfulness, it is important to let go of old views and wrong perceptions in order to remain an observer and one that accepts things as they are without opinion.

The Key Benefits of Mindfulness

Mindfulness has unlimited benefits that cut across all spheres of life. The overall key benefits of mindfulness are:

It heightens your level of awareness

It enables you to fully experience the present moment

It allows you to distinguish between the real you and your thoughts

It eliminates stress by making you an observer of your thoughts rather than someone that is constantly entangled by them

It supports attitudes that promote a satisfying life

It enables you to become more connected and in harmony with your being, the nature of human beings and the nature of things

It allows you to develop self-acceptance which yields self-contentment and compassion

It enables you to be fully engaged in day to day activities

It helps you enjoy life as it happens

It gives you a greater ability to deal with adverse situations

It increases your concentration and focus

It enables you to see that life is dynamic and that things change. Hence thoughts and feelings come and go

It gives you the freedom to experience calmness and peacefulness despite whatever is going on around you

It creates more balance in your emotions and reactions thus enabling you to be free from the chaos of emotional spikes and outbursts

It increases your awareness of the habits you've created in your thoughts and feelings.

It enables you to see thoughts as thoughts and feelings as feelings. This prevents you from getting caught up in them

It makes it more likely that you will make wise choices rather than ones based on stressful thought patterns that are fueled by confusion.

It allows you to remain free from the worries of the future and the regrets of the past

It allows you to maintain successful relationships because you develop the skill of communicating your emotions in a calm, professional way

It promotes self-insight, intuition, morality and fear modulation

Mindfulness improves physical health by:

Lowering blood pressure

Reducing chronic pain

Improving sleep

Relieving stress and worry

Alleviating gastrointestinal difficulties

Mindfulness can help treat:

Anxiety

Depression

Eating disorders (compulsive overeating, bulimia, anorexia)

Substance abuse

Obsessive-compulsive disorder

Chapter 2

The Importance of Living in the Present Moment

"The point of power is always in the present moment." - Louise Hay

The present moment refers to the moment that you are living right now. It is not the past and it is not the future. It is now.

You can't change the past and you can't control the future. You can however make the most of the present by staying consciously aware of the life that is yours to live in each moment.

According to author Eckhart Tolle, the present moment is all you really have. He writes "Realize deeply that the present moment is all you have. Make the NOW the primary focus of your life."

Unfortunately, most of us have a hard time appreciating the present because our "monkey minds," as Buddhists call them, jump from thought to thought like monkeys swinging from tree to tree. If we're not contemplating regrets of the past, we're worrying about the future.

Living in the present moment means living in acceptance

When you live in the present moment you live in acceptance. You accept life as it is right now, rather than how you wish it was. Being mindful allows you to live in the forgiveness of what you did or didn't do and it enables you to have peace, knowing that everything in your future will happen as it should.

Living in acceptance is also the key to alleviating mental stress. Stress can impact your health in many negative ways and it can also cloud your ability to make good decisions.

When you accept things as they are without judgment, you free yourself from the cycle of reasoning, resentment, anger, guilt and worry. When you free your mind from the mental stress these kinds of thoughts cause, you also free your body from the toxicity that these emotions produce.

Embrace your power to create

When you allow your thoughts to be overtaken by the past or future, you relinquish your personal power. Personal power is the ability to *choose* what you think about and what you do.

If your head is always stuck in the past or future, you are not exercising your power to create the kind of result you want in the present.

Contemplating past regrets or future worries only solidifies your fears and inadequacies. The subconscious mind loves images and *creates* on the basis of the pictures you give it. It does not differentiate between images and real situations.

For example, if in the present moment you use your thought power to create images of yourself failing a test, then chances are you will fail the test. Not because you don't have the knowledge to pass the test, rather it's because your subconscious mind spent countless days prior to the test solidifying failure through the images you gave it.

The present is the only moment you have to create change. If you want to change your life, you can only do that in the present moment by the thoughts you choose to think. When you consciously choose thoughts that can benefit you right now, you are using your personal power to create something good in every moment.

Chapter 3

Why Practice Mindfulness?

Mind Full, or Mindful? It's your choice.

Many people fail to practice mindfulness because they don't have a solid understanding of why they should practice it. It is only when they gain an understanding of why it is important that they will make it a part of their daily lives.

Why practice mindfulness?

Mindfulness enables you to:

Cultivate contentment

Build your self-confidence

Master your mind

Live in the present moment

Gain the power to be your best self

Enhance your quality of life

Cultivate contentment

Contentment is a state of happiness and satisfaction that exists when you are fully aware of the present moment. It is an awakening to the irrelevance of yesterday and tomorrow and an all embracing view of the importance of today.

When you practice mindfulness regularly you will be surprised how disconnected you become from your body (living in your mind). The more you separate yourself from the random thoughts running through your mind, the more peace and contentment you will have.

You will discover that mindfulness is an elevated, spirit-like state of being that functions above the frantic ways of the flesh.

Build your self-confidence

Without self-confidence, there is fear. Fear is derived from past experiences that are applied to the present and/or extrapolated into the future. Self-confidence exists when you feel adequate enough to fully experience the present moment.

Diminishing fear and escalating self-confidence depends on what thoughts you choose to think. Do you allow yourself to get wrapped up in the negative ramblings of your mind or do you pause, take a step back and take on the role of the observer, *choosing* to see the thoughts for what they are...*thoughts*.

Negative ramblings are simply habits that you've created. Mindfulness enables you to recognize the thoughts that no longer serve you and change them. This promotes a healthier sense of self-confidence.

Master your mind

Either you become the master of your mind or your mind becomes your master. In order for you to live a productive, purpose-filled life, you need to take control of your mind and refuse to be ruled by it.

Without mindfulness, this would be quite a daunting task. Mindfulness teaches you how to consciously control your thoughts so as to create the kind of experiences and reality that you want.

Live in the present moment

When you allow yourself to live in the present moment without littering your thoughts with past or future events that you can't do anything about, you empower yourself to deliberately create your life rather than letting life just happen to you.

Gain the 'power to be your best self'

Your mind follows a map that has been modeled by culture, traditions and past experiences. This map doesn't allow you the freedom to experience an uncharted path but rather a predetermined one.

The only way to escape this going nowhere, predetermined path is to liberate your mind from it through mindfulness.

Practicing mindfulness will enhance your quality of life

Practicing mindfulness raises your awareness and allows you to gain full control of your mind. When you are in control of your mind, you are in control of your life. This automatically enhances your quality of life because you can direct your life, moment by moment, toward what fulfills you most and makes you happy.

The Goal of Practicing Mindfulness

The goal of practicing mindfulness is to experience life now in its fullness. Experiencing life in its fullness means:

Living life fully in the present moment

Being consciously aware of life as you live it such that no part of it goes to waste via attachments

Allowing yourself to fully experience the present without undue reservations

Experiencing the freshness of every moment as a new moment that exists stain-free of the past and worry-free of the future

Chapter 4

How to Practice Mindfulness

"When you discover that all happiness is inside of you, the wanting and needing are over, and LIFE gets very exciting."

Byron Katie

Cultivating mindfulness is necessary in order to overcome worry and anxiety and access the natural wisdom that already resides in you. Understanding what mindfulness is all about is the first milestone to the way of mindfulness. Understanding why you should practice mindfulness is the second milestone. Learning how to practice mindfulness is the third milestone to the way of mindfulness.

Learning how to practice mindfulness involves three key levels:

Strategies

Tools for practicing mindfulness

Techniques

The key <u>strategies</u> for practicing mindfulness are:

Avoid anxiety

Focus your attention on the present moment

Enhance your power to attach and detach

Become nonjudgmental

Key <u>tools</u> for practicing mindfulness

The following is a mnemonic that will help you remember the various ways in which you can incorporate mindfulness into your day.

Rain

Stop

Walk/Run

Shower

Imagine being outside and suddenly encountering an unexpected heavy RAIN. What would you do? For a moment, you might STOP and acknowledge the fact that it's raining and then you would probably WALK/RUN for shelter. When you eventually arrive home you might SHOWER in order to feel clean and put together again.

Let's look at each of these words in detail to see how you can use each one to practice mindfulness daily.

<u>RAIN</u>

RAIN is an acronym for a four step process that was developed by a number of Buddhist teachers years ago in order to help people deal with intense emotions. The acronym RAIN is available to you anywhere. Whenever you experience a painful situation, you can find refuge in following this acronym to clear your mind of confusion and stress and systematically bring yourself to a place of truth and calm.

RAIN de-conditions the habitual ways in which you resist the present moment.

The four steps that work in tandem with the acronym RAIN are:

Recognize

Acknowledge

Investigate

Non-Identification

Recognize what is happening

Recognition is acknowledging what is true deep inside of you. It begins the second you recognize the emergence of a strong emotion. For example, you might recognize nervousness emerging but if you focus on the nervousness itself you might not recognize that the core of your physical response is actually a fear of failure.

When you recognize the emotion, it is important to ask yourself the question "What is happening inside of me right now?" Use your curiosity while focusing on the inner sensation. Try not to judge what you feel and instead observe and listen to what your body is telling you.

Allow life to be what it is

Allowing means to let the emotions, thoughts, and feelings simply be as they are. It is likely that you will cringe at the mere acceptance of a negative emotion but "allowing" the emotion, positive or negative, is extremely necessary for healing.

In order to soften the pain of the emotion you need to utter an encouraging word like "yes" or

"I consent." From the moment you do this you should feel a weakening of the emotions power over you. The more you continue to do this, the more the emotion will lose its power over you.

By consenting with the emotion, you avoid your usual resistance to the emotion. You begin to relax and accept the experience.

Investigate

It's possible that the first two steps of RAIN will be sufficient in providing a sense of peace and calm for you. If you feel you need to go further you can access your inner curiosity by investigating the emotion with kindness.

Do this by asking yourself "What does this feeling want from me?" "How am I feeling this in my body?" Hidden within the emotion you might find a painful sense of unworthiness or shame. It is important to become conscious of these hidden parts of an emotion in order to weed them out so that they no longer feed the belief that you are deficient.

The key steps involved in investigation are:

Observe – observe without attaching your identity to the emotion

31

Explore – explore the emotion without disturbing it

Learn – gather information and derive lessons from your exploration without attaching your opinions to it

Understand – understand the lessons learned during your exploration

Appreciate – appreciate that the emotion was necessary in order for you to learn and grow

Accept – accept the emotion as it is

<u>N</u>on-Identification

Non-identification means that who you really are is not defined by emotion. The N of the RAIN acronym requires no work, it simply expresses a result: the freeing realization of your natural awareness.

Non-identification helps to deflate the "same old story" your mind likes to regurgitate over and over. It promotes a clear understanding that the emotion is just a passing state of mind and doesn't define who you are.

Using RAIN allows you to sit back and watch the workings of your mind. Being a nonjudgmental observer of your mind allows you to grow in a deeper understanding of what fuels your anger, pain and fear.

STOP

When you find your mind racing with stress, use the STOP acronym:

Stop (what you are doing)

Take (a breath)

Observe (your thoughts, feelings and emotions)

Proceed (to that which ought to be done now)

Stop what you are doing

"Stop" is a powerful word in mindfulness. When you start experiencing stress, stop what you are doing and separate yourself from the activity for a moment.

Take a breath

Take a deep breath then breathe normally. Pay attention to the in and out motion of your breathing. If it helps, say "in" as you inhale and "out" as you exhale.

Observe your thoughts, feelings and emotions

By observing your thoughts, you can take note of what you are thinking. While observing, it is important to understand that your thoughts are not facts, they are merely thoughts. If a thought of inadequacy arises, simply acknowledge it, allow it to be what it is, and move on.

Name any emotion that you "see." Studies have proven that naming your emotions can provide a calming effect.

Proceed

Next, proceed to an activity that can support you in the moment and be an anti-dote to the emotion. This might include going for a walk, talking to a friend, or kicking your feet up.

WALK/RUN

The following mindfulness technique can be practiced while you are walking to work, running errands or going for a leisurely walk. Throughout your day, pay attention to whether you are rushing so much that you are missing out on the present moment.

Walk/Run mindfulness involves the following:

Appreciation

Grounding

Open Awareness

Mantra

Appreciation

As you walk, be thankful for your ability to walk. Think of those less fortunate than you that are confined to wheelchairs and don't have the luxury of walking like you do.

Grounding

Grounding is a way of intricately connecting with the physical act of walking. Focus your attention on your legs and feet as each foot rhythmically steps from heel to toe. Follow the motion of each foot as it repeats this process with every step.

Open Awareness

Walk a little slower and become aware of each of your senses one by one. Use your eyes to see what is around you as you walk. Use your ears to listen to the sounds. Taste the air moving in and out of your mouth. Feel the refreshing brush of the air on your face and smell the air.

Try also to be aware of all the senses at once. Drink in everything that you feel.

Mantra

While you walk, simply repeat a mantra that you enjoy. Focus your attention only on your steps and your mantra.

SHOWER

Practicing mindfulness while showering can reduce stress. Instead of thinking of everything on your "to-do" list while showering, try replacing that with your moment by moment experience.

Turn off your busy brain and drink in the smell of the soap. Feel the warm water gently beating on your face or on your back.

Tips for developing mindfulness

Understand that it will take a bit of time to train your brain to shut off its usual mental clatter and simply acknowledge the events of the present moment. The brain is use to *doing* something all the time, so be patient with it.

You may have to lead it back to what you want it to focus on several times. It can take a little while but it will learn the new habit you want it to learn. Just stay consistent and you'll get there.

Mindfulness and meditation go hand in hand. There are many meditation techniques that can help you develop your ability to focus and live in the present moment. For more information on how to meditate please see my Meditation for Beginners book. There is also a preview chapter of this book at the end of this book.

Chapter 5

Techniques for Practicing Mindfulness

"You can't stop the waves, but you can learn to surf." – Dr. Jon Kabat Zinn

In this chapter you will learn important exercises that you can use to practice mindfulness every day. Though the exercises vary, the goal is always to achieve a state of alert, focused relaxation by consciously observing thoughts and sensations without judgment. This redirects your focus to the present moment.

Mindful breathing

Mindful breathing involves being consciously aware of every inhale and exhale. As you focus your attention on your breathing, your rambling mind becomes silenced. Your breath becomes the object of your concentration. As you continue practicing mindful breathing, you gain more control of your life because you choose to live in the power of the moment.

In order to practice mindful breathing begin by slowly moving your attention onto the process of breathing. Follow each breath in and out by concentrating on what the air feels like coming into your body then out again. Pay attention to the expansion of your chest and abdomen as you inhale and the contraction of your body as the air is released. If you get distracted while doing this, simply recognize the distraction and then gently bring your attention back to your breathing.

When you end the excrcise of mindful breathing take some time to reflect on your experience and connect with the present moment.

One Minute Breathing

This excrcise is short and sweet and can be done at any point throughout your day. Start by taking some slow, deep relaxing breaths. Try to breathe deep in order to access your diaphragm.

When you feel that you have connected to the in/out motion of breathing look at your watch or clock. When the second hand reaches the 12 take a deep breath in and hold it while you slowly count to six. Slowly release the air, paying attention to every part of your slow exhale. Continue this for a full 60 seconds.

Use this exercise several times a day to restore your mind to peace, clarity and the present moment. Over time you can expand this exercise as you get use to the process.

Mindfulness meditation

Mindfulness meditation is practiced by sitting comfortably with your back straight and eyes closed. Pay attention to your breathing by listening to the in and out sound of your breath. If thoughts get in the way gently, in a non-judgemental way, bring them back to the act of breathing.

When you begin practicing mindfulness meditation, start by incorporating it into your life in small intervals − 5 or 10 minutes. This will be enough for you to begin learning this new habit.

As you practice this habit regularly and it becomes easier, you can slowly increase the amount of time you spend meditating. In each sitting, focus on your breathing and let yourself relax into every breath.

The goal of this meditation is simply to sit still and allow yourself to be comfortable with just being and calming your mind. The fact that

YOU sit down and calm YOUR mind is a strong self-empowerment tool for you.

The more you implement this habit, the more you can allow it to branch out into mindful awareness of feelings, thoughts and actions.

Sensory

Wherever you are, begin to notice sights, sounds, smells, touches and tastes. Drink in the experience of whatever is around you and entirely focus your attention on it.

Conscious observation

Take any object you have lying around the house and place it in your hand. Allow your attention to be entirely absorbed in the object. Simply observe it. Don't study it intellectually; rather see it for what it is.

This exercise should give you a heightened feeling of "nowness" as you take control of the present moment. You should feel your chattery thoughts of the past and future dissipate.

Conscious observation doesn't seem like much, but it is extremely powerful.

Mindful listening

Stop at any point throughout your day and really listen to the sounds that are going on around you.

Notice the sound of the computer humming. Listen to the birds chirping outside your window. Notice the sound of a car going by in the distance. Hear the sound of an airplane overhead.

Mindful listening offers a wonderful opportunity to experience serenity and peace in any given moment.

Mindfulness cues

This technique involves choosing certain environmental cues that will act as reminders to you to practice mindfulness the moment they occur.

For example, the sound of a plane flying by can trigger a response in you to immediately focus on your breathing. Washing your hands or seeing a cat or dog could also act as triggers.

There are no rules here. If the trigger works for you, use it.

Mindfulness cues are great at jolting you out of the autopilot state and bringing you back to the present moment.

Mindful eating

Mindful eating means paying attention to the entire experience of eating. Pay attention to the aroma of the food and savor the taste. Notice the colors of the food. Feel the texture of the food as you chew it. Hear the sounds of the food, the crunch or snap. Be 100% involved in the experience of eating. Avoid distractions in order to do this.

Mindful walking

The goal of mindful walking is to be aware of your environment and internal state (feelings, sensations, thoughts).

As you begin walking, be conscious of your feet connecting with the ground. Recognize your legs moving and pay attention to your muscles tensing and relaxing with every step. Notice the intensity of each step. Is it light or hard on the pavement?

Next, allow yourself to recognize your surroundings. Become aware of what you see, hear, feel, smell and taste. Feel the air on your skin and pay attention to what is going on around you.

As you remain conscious of your walking and surroundings, start to become aware of your thoughts and emotions. What are you thinking? What do you feel? Don't judge your thoughts and feelings; rather just recognize them for what they are.

If during your walk your thoughts start to wander to the past or future, gently acknowledge them and bring yourself back to the moment. Focus on each footstep again.

Don't get discouraged if your thoughts wander. This is completely normal in developing mindfulness. See it as an opportunity to develop your skill of refocusing your thoughts on the present moment.

Use STOP

Be proactive about consciously using STOP throughout your day. Check in with yourself at various points in the day to see if you are living in the present moment. If you are not, then apply the "P" in STOP and Proceed to some kind of action that will help support you in living in the now.

Give your brain a break

Instead of constantly being engaged in "doing something" like checking emails, making phone calls or getting work done, decide to give your brain a break. Look out the window for a minute and watch the clouds sailing by, the leaves falling, or the waves rolling in. Focus on your breathing and make your observance of nature a meditative experience. Try to completely engross yourself in the moment and enjoy what you see.

Ten seconds of concentration

Concentration is the door that shuts out mental chatter. In order to practice concentration, close your eyes and slowly count to ten. When your focus wanders, gently lead your thoughts back to number one.

Understand that it's normal to have this mindfulness technique go like this:

"One.....two.....three.....four.....what time was that meeting again? Oh, darn I broke my concentration."

"One.....two....three.....boy, it sure is hot out today. They said it's supposed to be sunny until Saturday. Oh shoot!

Don't worry. Mastering mindfulness is a process.

Spice up routine chores with mindfulness

Take one of your routine chores like cleaning and revamp the experience by entirely immersing yourself in it.

Take dusting for example. Focus on every detail of dusting, how the cloth feels on each surface, how the cloth sweeps across the surface and how dust is carried away with the cloth.

If it's sweeping, lose yourself in every stroke of the broom against the floor. If it's vacuuming, thoroughly involve yourself in the back and forth motion of the vacuum.

Gratitude and the magic of five

Take five things throughout the day that normally go unnoticed and recognize them as a blessing and something that you are grateful for.

For example, think of your senses, like your ability to see, smell, touch, taste, and hear. Imagine what life would be like without them. Take a moment to be grateful for your senses.

Continue this throughout the day with other things that you take for granted.

Being grateful always leads to a greater appreciation of life and restores balance. This alleviates stress, anxiety and worry and escalates a quiet sense of peace and happiness.

Chapter 6

How Mindfulness is Important for Your Personal Development

"The realization that you have control and influence over your own life is a key concept you will need to understand to practice mindfulness."

– Janet Louise Stephenson

Practicing mindfulness makes you a better person. It nurtures your personal development and allows you to peel away layers of incorrect thinking that don't serve you well and replace them with layers of healing and truth that nurture your wellbeing. Following is a list of ways in which mindfulness can help you become better.

Raises your conscious awareness

Mindfulness teaches you to raise your conscious awareness. Raising your conscious awareness is a choice to live at a higher, more spiritual level. When you connect with your inner Spirit, all the information you receive on a daily basis is filtered through sensory impressions, rather than emotional reactions. This provides a deeper, truer understanding of the situation and prohibits you from making decisions based on false perceptions that are clouded by emotion.

Changes your focus

It is your responsibility to take control of your mind. If you let it think whatever it wants to think, it will relentlessly and anxiously pace back and forth like a caged animal reasoning, worrying, tossing around ideas all day long. The only way to tame the wildness of your mind is to intentionally focus it to what you want it to focus on.

Alleviates baggage

Mindfulness enables you to release potential grudges before they have a chance to stew and fester. Grudges breed resentment. Without resentment, you free yourself of the baggage that is created by guilt, shame, regret and hurt.

Brings forth your creative self

When you live in unity with Spirit you open the door to creativity. Inspiration, freshness and uniqueness is all contained in Spirit. It is impossible to be fully alive without a connection to your creative self.

Frees you from self-judgment

The way you judge others is always in direct proportion to how you judge yourself. When you raise your conscious awareness you begin to recognize your own self-judgment. Recognizing how you judge yourself is a gateway to freeing yourself from self-judgment.

Judging yourself and others is a waste of time and completely fruitless. Seeing the truth of who you are rather than beating yourself up or blaming others is the way to freedom.

Nurtures self-acceptance

As you connect with your breathing and become an observer of your own thoughts without censoring them, you accept yourself. If you judge your own thoughts or censor them, they will settle deep within you and you won't be able to learn and grow.

If you accept your thoughts without judgment then you will be able to put your finger on what it is that is disrupting your peace and causing you stress and anxiety. Often the only way to say goodbye to something is to first say hello to it.

Weeds out the negative

Mindfulness doesn't stop negative thoughts or feelings but it does make you question whether they are true or not. Much of life is about perception, how you perceive events. Without mindfulness, negative thoughts can turn into road blocks that stop you from reaching your full potential. Mindfulness teaches you to choose your perceptions based on truth and to see events for what they really are.

Enhances your psychological wellbeing

Psychological wellbeing is achieved when your self-awareness and self-esteem are optimized to such an extent that you can experience freedom and fulfillment. It is by experiencing freedom and fulfillment that you become happy.

Chapter 7

How Mindfulness is Important in Your Relationships

"If you correct your mind, the rest of your life will fall into place."

– Lao Tzu

All too often, relationships end up being a minefield of old habits, baggage, unrealistic expectations and misunderstandings. Most of us enter relationships for companionship and to build a connection with someone special. Our intentions are sweet, honest and good. Yet why is it that so many of them go sour?

According to neuropsychologist, Marsha Lucas "Autopilot is the big enemy in relationships." Functioning on autopilot means reacting to situations the same way we did as kids in our child/parent relationship. Even as adults we tend to mirror the same actions we had as kids." Why is this?

The reason is because most of the wiring in our brains that affect relationships happens very early on in life. For example, fearful events become etched in the emotional part of our brain as kids. Marsha Lucas says that "In the realm of relationships, any fearful or painful or potentially unsafe memories of long-ago relationship experiences are in standby mode, ready to 'help' you avoid being hurt today."

This early wiring can cause:

...repeated discrepancies in relationships

...the infliction of certain embedded beliefs or unexpected ideals onto the other person

...the repetition of unnecessary behaviors that lead to the same arguments over and over again.

Luckily, previous mental wiring is reversible. As adults we are able to make new connections that can benefit us instead of hurt us and others.

Mindfulness enables us to rewire our brains in order to make our relationships long-lasting, fruitful and loving. When we apply mindfulness to relationships we strengthen and nurture them.

The benefits of mindfulness in relationships

According to Marsha Lucas, "mindfulness can help us break out of the negative knee-jerk reactions we bring to relationships"

Becoming mindful allows us to accept responsibility for our thoughts and actions. Often in relationships it is easy to blame the other person for being difficult, not listening to us and not understanding us. When you start taking responsibility for your actions you weed out guilt and blame. This enables you to begin to put an end to repetitive dramas and reach a more intimate, meaningful place with your partner and with yourself.

Mindfulness helps you:

...control your emotions

...observe your reactions to things in order to change them

...manage your body's reactions to certain events

...calm your fears and anxieties

These are all necessary ingredients for healthy relationships.

With a newly rewired brain that sees things for what they really are, your initial reaction of nitpicking something about your partner will be overridden by a loving conversation that nurtures each of your needs.

Mindfulness helps your brain make choices in the present moment that serve you and the relationship that you are in.

Mindfulness allows you to be fully present to enjoy and appreciate being with friends and family. When you immerse yourself into the experience of really *being* with others, you create quality time with them.

Mindfulness makes you a better listener. When you are living in the present moment you can really listen to what the other person is saying. This gives that person a feeling that what they are saying is important and shows them that you care about them and what they are saying.

Mindfulness makes you more empathetic. Showing empathy is the act of understanding the other person's condition from their perspective. When you put yourself in their shoes it expresses concern and care for that person.

Mindfulness makes you better at communicating. When you are aligned with conscious awareness of your own thoughts and feelings it allows you to express your experiences more clearly.

Being more mindful and present to the truth in a situation stops you from applying past misconceptions and future suffering to it. This enables you to avoid a lot of conflict and remain closer and connected to your partner.

When a couple works together in a mindful way to nurture their relationship, there is a lot of understanding, compassion, love and heart that is applied to that relationship.

Dr. Jon Kabat-Zinn said "When we know ourselves, we become stronger in our relationships." Mindfulness enables you to observe yourself at a deeper, truer level in order to weed out your bad habits and replace them with good ones. When you do this you help not only yourself but your relationships.

Chapter 8

How Mindfulness is Important in Your Work and Business

"Be happy in the moment, that's enough. Each moment is all we need, not more."

– Mother Teresa

Work and business are two things that preoccupy our adult lives. Workplaces and business environments can cause us stress. However, most of these stresses can be avoided through mindfulness.

The importance of mindfulness while working

Key strategies in maintaining a sense of mindfulness while working are to:

Avoid anxiety

Focus your attention on the present moment

Use your power to attach and detach

Be nonjudgmental

These will go a long way in ensuring that your work doesn't become a source of misery but rather a source of joy and happiness.

Avoid anxiety – You can avoid anxiety by not worrying about what your boss will say or won't say about the task you are working on. Seek personal satisfaction in your accomplishment. Stop trying to please your boss. Instead focus on doing your personal best.

Focus your attention on the present moment – Do not focus on your past failures and avoid focusing on the negatives that could happen tomorrow. These kinds of thoughts only serve to disturb your focus from the present moment. They also promote stress and worry.

Use your power to attach and detach – Learn to schedule your tasks and focus on doing the right task at the right moment. When you are working on one task, don't start thinking of the next task. Also don't contemplate the task you just finished. Understand that there is a time to work and a time for leisure. During your leisure time avoid thoughts of work and let yourself fully enjoy your leisure time.

Be nonjudgmental – Don't judge your colleagues, supervisors and juniors.

The importance of mindfulness while doing business

Just as you can apply the strategies mentioned above to maintaining a sense of mindfulness at work, you can also apply them to business by:

Avoiding anxiety – Let business happen in the now. Don't panic about potentially missing your target for the day. Simply focus on the present moment and avoid worrying about things that are beyond your control.

Focusing your attention on the present moment – Be entirely of service to your customers by addressing their needs as best as you can in the present moment.

Using your power to attach and detach – Value your customers. If they have chosen to shop your store, thank them and provide them with the best service. If they reference buying product from a competitor, understand that they are just exercising their ability to attach and detach. Don't take it personally. Rather, be courteous and tell them you appreciate their business.

Being nonjudgmental – Don't judge your customers, employees or your suppliers.

Chapter 9

How Mindfulness is Important in Your Everyday Life

"If you want others to be happy, practice compassion. If you want to be happy, practice compassion."

– Dalai Lama

Life can be messy, competitive and hard. That is exactly why it's important to value compassion. Being compassionate to oneself is what mindfulness is all about. It is the antidote to losing your sense of peace and joy on a daily basis.

In the pre-flight instructions on a plane, flight attendants will tell passengers to secure their own oxygen mask first before assisting others. It is important to apply this to your life as well. The more you learn how to be compassionate to yourself first, the more you can show compassion to others.

According to recent scientific findings, researchers have discovered that being happy is a state of mind that starts with your self-view. Their theory states the following:

When we feel a deep sense of gratitude toward ourselves, appreciating our good nature, and showing ourselves love, self-worth and self-compassion, we are more capable of meeting life's challenges with success and grace, thus minimizing anxiety, worry and depression. There's simply no chance of enjoying life without first generating self-compassion.

Practicing mindfulness enables you to develop a strong sense of self-compassion. This creates happiness on a daily basis.

Think of self-compassion as the hub of everything else in your life. When your hub is solid, your life is solid. It is your self-view that taints everything you are and everything that you do.

Mindfulness allows you to establish a hub that you can build a happy life on. Until you decide to practice mindfulness on a daily basis your mind will rule you and overtake your life. It is only when you learn how to live mindfully that you will be able to shape your own destiny, alleviate stress and worry and live a happy and peaceful life.

Conclusion

Congratulations on finishing the book!

I'm passionate about mindfulness and I hope this book has provided you with the necessary information you need to apply the transformational benefits of mindfulness to your life today!

I know first-hand how powerful mindfulness is and I want to reach as many people as I can with this book in order to share the life-giving benefits of mindfulness.

So...if you enjoyed this book, please tell your friends about it or purchase a copy for them as a gift. Helping someone else achieve inner peace and happiness is a wonderful thing.

I've included a preview of my *Meditation for Beginners* book in the next section. Meditation and mindfulness go hand in hand. If you enjoy what you read, you can pick up a copy of my book on Amazon.

Thank you again for purchasing my book. I sincerely hope that the information I've provided in this book changes your life for the better.

Preview of

Meditation for Beginners

How to Relieve Stress, Anxiety and Depression and Return to a State of Inner Peace and Happiness

Yesenia Chavan

Available on Amazon

Chapter 1

What is Meditation?

*Meditation is the dissolution of thoughts in
Eternal awareness or Pure consciousness
without objectification, knowing without
thinking, merging finitude in infinity.*
- Voltaire

In order to understand what meditation is, it is
first necessary to look at life from the
standpoint of what we as human beings can
control. Do we have complete control over
every aspect of our lives or is our control
limited?

At first you might be tempted to say that you do
have complete control over every aspect of your
life, but when you dig a little deeper you will
find that the only two things that you can
completely control in life are your thoughts and
actions. That's it. Most things are simply
beyond your control.

Fortunately, the power to take responsibility
for your personal state of mind *is* something
you have control over. Therefore, you have the
ability to change your state of mind for the
better.

According to Buddhism this is an important thing that you can and should do for yourself. In fact, Buddhism believes that taking complete control of your state of mind is the only real antidote to worry, anxiety, fear, confusion, stress and frustration.

Meditation is a way of transforming your mind. By using techniques that encourage and promote concentration, positive feelings, clarity, a relaxed state, and a calm way of seeing the truth in all things, you can improve your mental and physical well being.

Meditation also offers an opportunity to get in touch with your mind on an intricate spiritual level in order to discover its habits and patterns. It is one of the most effective ways to cultivate new, positive and fulfilling ways of being.

Meditation exists beyond the mind

Meditation is a state of thoughtless awareness. It is not about effort or doing, rather it is simply a state of awareness.

According to Indian mystic, guru and spiritual teacher, Osho "All that the mind is capable of *doing* and *achieving* is not relevant when it comes to meditation – meditation is something beyond the mind. The mind is absolutely helpless when it comes to meditation."

Osho goes on to say that "The mind cannot penetrate meditation; where mind ends, meditation begins."

You and I have been taught to believe that everything can be done with the mind. So, when it comes to meditation, our natural inclination is to start thinking in terms of techniques, methods and what we can *do* to maximize our meditational experience.

It makes sense that we would think this way because so many things in life validate the use of the mind in getting what we want. We have been raised with the belief that "if you just put your mind to it, you can do anything." There is truth to that, yet the only thing that the mind cannot "do" is meditate.

Meditation techniques will teach you *how* to take control of and connect with your mind, but the necessity of that control only pertains to the degree in which it allows you to free yourself from your mind.

Meditation is your true nature. It is your being. It is fully you and it can only be entered into through the emptying of your mind. As Osho teaches "Meditation is not an achievement – it is something that already exists in you, it is your nature. It is there waiting for you – just turn inward and it is available. You have been carrying it always."

Meditation therefore is the simple process of removing your attention from current conditions and circumstances which when focused on too regularly fragment and cloud your perceptions.

When you allow for clear, unadulterated levels of conscious awareness to occur you access the spiritual being inside of you. This Spirit being is superior to your human mind and physical body and offers guidance and peace that you are unable to achieve at a human level.

As you consistently and patiently learn how to empty your mind, the deepened focus and concentration that you immerse yourself in will slowly create in you an intensely peaceful, powerful, clear and energised state of mind.

This spiritually energised state of mind is your intrinsic, Spirit nature that can guide and lead you in Truth and cause a transformative effect that will give you a new understanding of life.

About the Author

"A stress free, healthy and positive life is available to anyone that is willing to change."

Living a life of peace, great health and happiness shouldn't feel like something that is available to everyone but you. There is a whole world of limitless possibility out there but only YOU can make it a reality in your own life.

My name is Yesenia Chavan. I use to be stressed-out, overweight, unhappy and desperate to live the 'great life' I dreamed of. There were many years that I lived as a victim of circumstance completely oblivious to the fact that I had the power to choose the kind of life I wanted to live.

One day, completely stressed-out by my situation, I made a decision to learn everything I could on inner peace, happiness and taking control of my life. I devoured every book I could get my hands on and eagerly applied everything I learned to my life.

Slowly I started experiencing more peace, health and happiness than I ever had before. For the first time in my life I felt that I was in complete control of my destiny. Life became an exciting, rich, beautiful playground that I couldn't wait to enjoy every day. Positive things started happening for me. I hit my goal weight, started living my passion and tripled my income. It still amazes me today how one quality decision could transform my life so drastically.

Now I'm on a mission to share what I've learned in a straight-forward, simple, to-the-point kind of way that will enable you to transform your life in a short amount of time. You're busy and the last thing you need is to wade through a 500 page book on how to find peace, release stress, get healthy and live happy. That's why my books are concise, easy to read and aim to answer your most pressing questions.

Everything I write comes from the heart and my goal with every book is to help you live the stress free, happy life you were meant to live.

When I'm not writing I enjoy yoga, long walks, spending time at the beach and reading.

Thank you for exploring my books. My hope is that they will be a light for you as so many books were to me.

Made in the USA
San Bernardino, CA
10 October 2016